Wellbeing
Wombat

Pippa Bird

In the Australian bush, there lived a wise and caring wombat named Warren. He was known for his deep understanding of emotions and his ability to help his friends feel better.

sniffle

One day, Warren was cleaning around his burrow when he heard his friend, Piper Potoroo, crying nearby.

He quickly waddled over to her.
"Piper, what's the matter?" He asked gently.

"I feel so scared because I've lost my way home. I don't know what to do." Piper replied.
"How will I get home? What if I'm lost forever?!"

Warren nodded sympathetically. "It's okay to feel scared, Piper. Everyone feels scared sometimes."

"Let's take a deep breath together and then we can find your way home."

Piper wiped her eyes and looked up at Warren.
He continued, "I know you want to get home, and I know that
you're afraid, but your emotional wellbeing is most important
right now."

"What does that
mean?" the
potoroo asked.

Warren thought for a moment, closing his eyes before responding, "It means that it's important for you to be calm and have your thoughts collected before you do anything else."

"Oh, what happens if I ignore
my emotional wellbeing?"
pressed the potoroo.

"Your feelings will remain a mess, you will not be able to think clearly and you may stay lost," answered Warren.

Piper thought for a moment. As she started pacing and rocking, her anxious feelings started to amplify.

Warren noticed Piper was not okay. He reached his arm out toward her, taking her hand in his.

Piper looked around the bush.

"Piper, can you name five things you can see?" asked Warren.

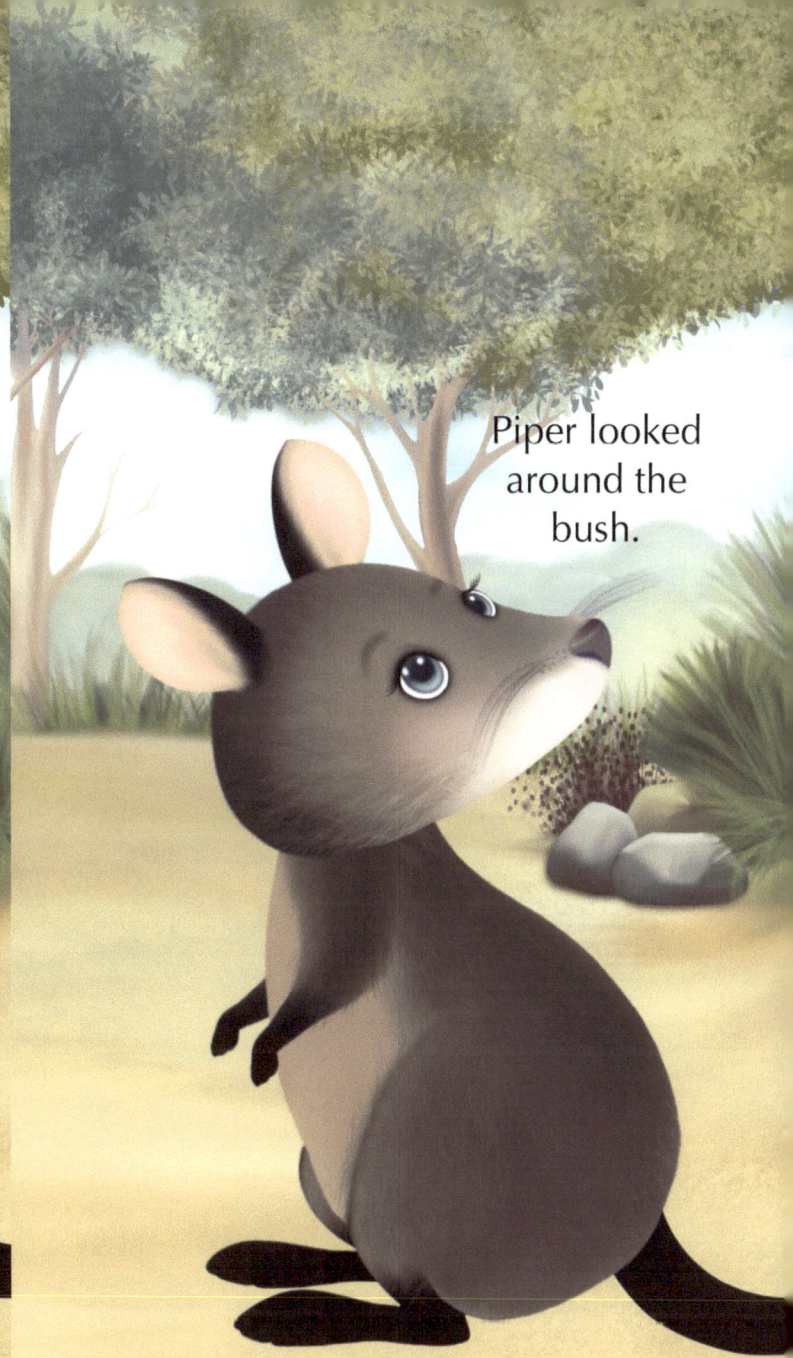

"I can see a tree, a leaf, the blue sky, a stick and the sun."

"Great. How do you feel right now?" asked the wombat.

"I feel like I want to keep playing," smiled Piper.

A large smile spread across
Warren's face. Piper had
forgotten why she was upset,
and was now focused on
Warren's game.

"Let's keep going. Can you find
four things you can touch?"
continued the wombat, leading
Piper through the bush.

Piper hopped around the bush floor,
touching odds and ends.

"I can touch this piece of bark."

"And this huge rock."

"I can touch this soft dirt."

The potoroo hopped over to a patch of grass and felt it lush beneath her feet. "And, this green grass."

Warren continued to watch his friend, "Now, can you name three things you can hear? You might need to take a deep breath and sit still for this one."

Piper stood still, took a deep breath and cast her ears to the bush around her.

"I can hear a gentle breeze rustle the leaves in the trees. I can hear the soft babbling of a nearby stream. And I can hear the distant laughter of a kookaburra."

"Perfect, Piper. Can you notice two things that you can smell?"

"Smell? Like this familiar bottlebrush over here," she said, following her nose and moving further into the bush.

Warren smiled, "Exactly. Now there's just one more thing. It's a little different."

"And those eucalyptus leaves?" she asked.

"What is one thing you can softly say to yourself, to make your heart settle like the leaves falling from the trees?"

The potoroo looked around her, a familiar warmth spread across her body.

She sighed in relief, "I'm home."

"Oh, Warren. How did you
do that?" she beamed.

"You did it, Piper. Your body knew which way to go to get home,
all you had to do was clear your mind, centre your feelings and
take a moment to calm yourself. You should be so proud."

Warren smiled cheerfully, "I'm glad, little potoroo. Always remember that your emotional wellbeing is the most important."

"Thank you, my special friend. I will remember this day if I ever find myself lost again."

Calm Kangaroo series by Pippa Bird. Available on Amazon.

Calm Kangaroo
Mindfulness Alphabet
Written & Illustrated by Pippa Bird

Quiet Quokka
Written & Illustrated by Pippa Bird

Positive Platypus
Soula's Self-image

Co-regulating Koala
Lost and Found

Unwind with Calm Kangaroo
Written & Illustrated by Pippa Bird

Positive Platypus
Posy's Special Find

Co-regulating Koala
Tumbling Tower

Co-regulating Koala
The Loud Crack

Wobbly Roo
Pippa Bird

Logical Lyrebird
Pippa Bird

Hop by Hop
Pippa Bird

Hop, Skip, Rest

Elated Emu
Pippa Bird

Corroborate Cockatoo
Pippa Bird

Kind Kookaburra
Pippa Bird

Timely Tarantula
Pippa Bird

Nonsense Numbat
Pippa Bird

Polite Python
Pippa Bird

Bully Bilby
Pippa Bird

Empathetic Echidna
Pippa Bird

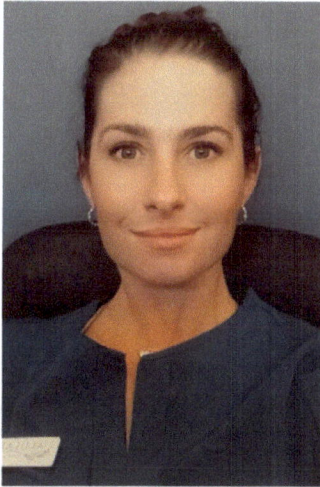

About the Author
Pippa Bird is a former Mental Health Therapist in Private Practice Alula Blu Counselling Services, in regional NSW

Pippa holds a Bachelor in Psychology, a Diploma in Counselling, and a Diploma in Graphic Design, with a primary focus on illustration.

Calm Kangaroo

CALM KANGAROO is a backronym title for a children's mental and emotional well-being program. An initiative designed to educate children about mental health and foster a learning journey of emotional intelligence, resilience and cultivate an open mind through the benefits of reading well-being books, leading to the most important discussions and ideas.

CALM KANGAROO focuses on Curating, Advocating & Leading Mindfulness, & its mission to Kindle Awareness, Nurture Growth, Amplify Resilience, & Orchestrate Open-minds.

www.ingramcontent.com/pod-product-compliance
Lightning Source LLC
LaVergne TN
LVHW072112070426
835509LV00003B/129